MUSCLE CARS

THE FIRST AMERICAN SUPERCARS

Colin Romanick

SHIRE PUBLICATIONS

Published in Great Britain in 2012 by Shire Publications
Ltd, Midland House, West Way, Botley, Oxford OX2 0PH,
United Kingdom.

44-02 23rd Street, Suite 219, Long Island City, NY 11101,
USA.

E-mail: shire@shirebooks.co.uk   www.shirebooks.co.uk

© 2012 Colin Romanick.

All rights reserved. Apart from any fair dealing for the
purpose of private study, research, criticism or review, as
permitted under the Copyright, Designs and Patents Act,
1988, no part of this publication may be reproduced,
stored in a retrieval system, or transmitted in any form or
by any means, electronic, electrical, chemical, mechanical,
optical, photocopying, recording or otherwise, without the
prior written permission of the copyright owner.
Enquiries should be addressed to the Publishers.

Every attempt has been made by the Publishers to secure
the appropriate permissions for materials reproduced in
this book. If there has been any oversight we will be happy
to rectify the situation and a written submission should be
made to the Publishers.

A CIP catalogue record for this book is available from the
British Library.

Shire Library no. 668.   ISBN-13: 978 0 74781 096 4

Colin Romanick has asserted his right under the
Copyright, Designs and Patents Act, 1988, to be identified
as the author of this book.

Designed by Tony Truscott Designs, Sussex, UK
and typeset in Perpetua and Gill Sans.

Printed in China through Worldprint Ltd.

12 13 14 15 16   10 9 8 7 6 5 4 3 2 1

COVER IMAGE
GTOs saw the introduction of a semifastback in 1968 that
carried over into the next year. Minor revisions to the
front and rear were overshadowed by the introduction of
Ram Air V and a model called "The Judge." Ram Air-
equipped cars could clear the quarter mile in less than
twelve seconds.

TITLE PAGE IMAGE
While most 1969 Plymouth Road Runners were equipped
with a 383-cubic inch engine, a 426-cid Hemi was
available. Fewer than a thousand Road Runners had a Hemi
under the hood, and only six were convertibles.

CONTENTS PAGE IMAGE
General Motors offered muscle cars in each of their
divisions with the exception of Cadillac. The Pontiac GTO,
Chevrolet Chevelle SS, Buick Skylark GS, and Oldsmobile
442 were featured in several ads together and had
established followings by 1968.

ACKNOWLEDGEMENTS
I am grateful to my wife for her support in my automotive
pursuits and to my father for sharing his passion for the
automobile with me. The great majority of the vintage
advertisements are from the collection of Brent Romanick,
while the ones on pages 15–32 are from the collection of
Clay Drnec, who provided additional guidance on
technical aspects of the book. The image on page 32 is
from the archives of the William J. Clinton Library. The
photographs on pages 59–60 are from the U.S. National
Archives & Records Administration. A special thanks to
Passing Lane Motors for the use of the image on page 21,
and to RK Motors Charlotte for the images on pages 18,
20, 22, 27, 34, 46, 48, 62, and 63. All other photographs
belong to the author.

Shire Publications is supporting the Woodland Trust, the UK's leading woodland conservation charity, by funding the dedication of trees.

ORIGINS

IN 1955, the debut of Chrysler's C-300 embodied the desires of many and pointed to an increasing horsepower competition between American automakers. Mating a powerful engine to a four-passenger coupe was at the heart of what would become a muscle car revolution. The C-300 was powered by a 331-cubic-inch-diameter (cid) Hemi V8 engine producing 300 horsepower (hp). This would make the C-300 the most powerful factory-produced passenger car when released. Chryslers were (and still are) known for being luxurious, and the C-300 was no exception. This luxury and performance came at a 1955 base price of $4,929, which limited production to just 1,725 examples built.

The end of World War II brought many servicemen home to families and sweethearts. These younger "baby boomers" grew up in a period of great economic wealth. They had more than any generation before them, and they felt special. A desire for cutting-edge technology and uniqueness drove their buying habits. This redefined the way Americans looked at the automobile.

Extremely conservative executives at the "Big Three" automakers in the United States (Chrysler, Ford, General Motors) were content with the status quo of automotive design. American automotive designs of the 1950s focused on the influence of the jet age. Many cars featured target or bomb sight hood ornaments, large upright fins as part of the fenders, and exhaust pipes that protruded through the rear bumper. Only the rise of younger executives and engineers would change the situation. Men like John Z. DeLorean, Harley Earl, and Zora Arkus-Duntov would lead the charge for greater performance and designs appealing to the relatively untapped youth market. Until their time, performance was secondary to plush amenities and a soft ride that would absorb miles of rough roads with aplomb. The C-300 was an effort to merge the two views, but it was not the first.

America's first true sports car, the Corvette, sped onto the road in late 1953. Harley Earl's creation was introduced at the GM Motorama in 1953 with a standard "Blue Flame" in-line 6-cylinder engine. It was not until the 1955 model year that a V8 engine was offered as an option. Arkus-Duntov,

Opposite:
The Studebaker Golden Hawk may have featured a 352-cid V8, but, like the Chrysler C-300, it was luxurious and expensive. This was attractive and obtainable by middle-aged adults with families but not younger buyers.

known as the "father" of the Corvette, helped introduce the V8 option. He recognized the need for performance and assisted in coaxing a conservative company into one with youth appeal.

The Corvette was marketed to returning veterans who desired the small sporty cars they had seen while stationed in Europe. Many British and Italian sports cars were already being imported and finding their way onto American roads and racetracks. However, they lacked the power of a V8 engine and had the limitation of only being two-seaters, like the Corvette. In addition, the all-composite body and $2,774 price of the Corvette made it ineligible to be a muscle car. Although the Corvette possessed V8 power, which improved performance, it still did not qualify as the first muscle car.

Defining a muscle car is no simple task. Ask any two automotive enthusiasts, and you will get different answers on a definition. The strictest definition does incorporate several key elements, though. Only intermediate-sized coupes and later convertibles that were standard production vehicles qualify. They must be powered by the largest capacity, highest performance version of a V8 engine in a particular manufacturer's model. Some consider 350 cubic inches and above the requirement for muscle car status. A stout drive train, brakes, and suspension aid in managing the brutal power.

The rising youth market wanted more performance from their cars than the previous generation. Making these cars affordable meant less opulence, which appealed to the mature drivers who remembered the Ford Model As of yesteryear.

European cars made a lasting impression on those Americans who had seen military service in Europe. British makers like MG and Triumph had success in the postwar years that the Corvette would share.

Chevrolet's Corvette debuted in 1953, but it was not until 1955 that a V8 was available. In 1957, fuel injection became available, which raised the price of this two-seater sports car even more beyond a young buyer's reach.

The smoky burnouts associated with muscle cars would not be possible without the power being transmitted to the drive wheels. Therefore, most high-performance models moved the manual transmission shifter to the floor

Detroit makes the car...

Hurst makes the driving more fun!

Detroit points the way in '64 with a fabulous choice of power plant and transmission options for performance driving. And if you really want to drive a new '64, put a famous Hurst stick shift on the floor. Hurst transmission controls and your skill deliver all the performance capability your car offers—plus exciting, quick, smooth shifting. Choose the Hurst Competition Plus 4-speed shifter for performance driving at its best—or one of the superb 3-speed units. All Hurst shifters are so ruggedly built they carry an unconditional guarantee for the life of your installation. They are available for all popular cars at leading speed shops everywhere. They are widely imitated, but never equaled—so insist on Hurst. See your local speed shop dealer or write to us today.

HURST PERFORMANCE PRODUCTS, INC., Glenside, Pa.

HURST

and offered four speeds instead of the standard three forward speeds. An additional gear allowed for brisker acceleration and a higher top speed. Some drag racers, or "diggers," preferred the heavy-duty automatic transmissions for quicker shifts that would not miss a gear when shifting.

Power and torque were sent to the rear axle, which transmitted power to the ground. Manufacturers offered different rear-axle gears, which could range from a high ratio for brisk acceleration to lower for more comfortable highway cruising. Limited-slip differentials helped to minimize wheel spin and transmit power to the ground. Chevrolet's Positraction is one of the most famous limited-slip differentials. The downside to "posi," as it is commonly known, is that it can change the handling of a vehicle. While providing additional traction for acceleration, it also can induce oversteer in tight corners.

Increased power necessitated better braking and suspension designs. Brakes on most cars consisted of drum brakes "all around." More powerful disc brakes would become standard on the front of more high-performance models, especially muscle cars. This would bring 3,000 pounds or more of car to a stop in a reasonable but not exceptional stopping distance. Suspensions would be strengthened with stiffer springs and attachment points as well as wider-profile tires for better traction and cornering.

All of these performance modifications would come at a price. Affordability was part of the muscle car formula. This is the reason why many muscle cars do not have many of the options considered standard equipment today. A large percentage did not have air conditioning, interior or trunk carpeting, power steering, or even a radio. Instead, many owners settled for a Spartan interior with a heater and vinyl floor mats, often purchasing their own tachometer, which may or may not have been offered as standard equipment. Limiting options on muscle cars was done not only to keep sticker prices lower, but also because less weight meant faster quarter-mile times and increased overall performance.

A muscle car is defined as much by its performance as by its appearance. The aggressive look of a muscle car is comprised of several elements. The most obvious is the "Coke-bottle" shape of the body. While not the most aerodynamic style, it does create an ominous presence. A narrow front flows

Opposite: George Hurst cofounded Hurst-Campbell in 1958 and was a supplier of performance products to several U.S. manufacturers. Hurst made such a reputation with drag racers for his great shifters and clutches that many of his products were original equipment on many muscle cars.

The Magnum wheel can be found on many muscle cars. The wide rims and performance Wide-Oval tires from Firestone provided enhanced grip and were incorporated into suspension package offerings from manufacturers.

to a larger rear able to accommodate an increased wheel and tire size combination. So called "impact colors" offered by manufacturers helped to make the muscle cars stand out from the crowd. These colors were not standard and are equally shocking when seen today as back in the day. Names such as "Banana Yellow," "Panther Pink," "Plum Crazy," and "Sublime Green" reflect the nature of these colors. In some cases, the bumpers could be painted the body color instead of the usual chrome. Special badges also would adorn the bodywork, identifying the special model in addition to the engine displacement. Decals and stripes added aviation or racing influences to many muscle cars. Some of the decals incorporated engine sizes or the name of the model.

Being seen and not heard did not apply to muscle cars. Another characteristic of muscle cars was a dual exhaust. A dual exhaust system allows for less back pressure and increased horsepower. Some manufacturers even built in devices to allow the exhaust note to be changed or for increased volume. If a shocking paint color or racing decals did not get attention, the roar of a V8 certainly would.

All of these characteristics that define a muscle car did not occur overnight. The beginning would be followed by years of research and

1970 Dodge Challengers in R/T trim are some of the most desirable muscle cars today. Fewer than a thousand R/T convertibles were produced and even fewer in the high-impact color of Plum Crazy.

Engine displacements are proudly displayed on any muscle car in the form of badges and decals. In this case, a 1967 Chevelle's badge announces the presence of a 396 Turbo-Jet under the hood to any and all competitors.

development resulting in the ultimate car. The story of the first true muscle car can be traced to a particular model that quickly became known by its nickname, the "Goat."

The obvious Coke-bottle shape can be seen looking down the flank of this 1969 Dodge Charger R/T. Notice the bumble bee stripe and R/T decal on the rear portion of the car.

MUSCLE MATTERS

WHEN MOST PEOPLE think of John Z. DeLorean, they think of his gull wing-inspired, Hollywood time-traveling DMC-12 rather than his earlier automotive exploits. His own DeLorean Motor Company was a short-lived and unfortunate end to an otherwise fantastic automotive career. As an up-and-coming engineer, DeLorean had worked at both Chrysler and Packard, but it was at GM's Pontiac division where he would make automotive history.

It was General Manager S. E. "Bunkie" Knudsen who was given the job of reviving the Pontiac brand in 1956. Knudsen wanted to build fun cars that would appeal to younger people and shed the old "Indian Chief" image for good. An arrowhead would replace the bust of the Indian chief as Pontiac's logo in 1959. Bringing on enthusiasts like DeLorean and proven winners like Pete Estes generated quick results. Estes had performed miracles at another GM division—Oldsmobile—and Knudsen was correct that he would do the same for Pontiac. Introducing the Wide-Track design and adding Tri Power carburetion or even the optional Rochester fuel injection infused life into Pontiac and gave it a hip appeal.

With Knudsen's move to Chevrolet in 1961, Estes was promoted to general manager of Pontiac, and DeLorean became the automaker's youngest chief engineer, at age thirty-six. It was during this time that DeLorean began his "what if" sessions on Saturday mornings at the divisional proving grounds facility in Milford, Michigan. He would typically invite top-level engineers, veteran sales staff, and even personal friends to discuss and review various projects and ideas.

During one of these sessions in early 1963, Bill Collins, assistant chief engineer, and Russ Gee, a top engine man, were looking over a Pontiac Tempest with DeLorean. The Tempest was a prototype and even had primer on it. It was Collins who made the suggestion that a 389-cid V8 would probably fit in the place of the usual 326-cid V8. Gee and DeLorean both liked the idea, and Collins had the car ready for the next session. The Tempest was a hit, and they continued to make refinements to the car. In the end, the

Opposite: Chrysler chose the 1964 Plymouth Belvedere with its lightweight body to showcase the new 426 Hemi. Hemi-equipped Belvederes were a terror on the track, and race versions came with a disclaimer and no warranty.

Right: This Pontiac GTO is equipped with a Hurst Dual-Gate shifter, allowing for normal automatic mode on one side of the gate and slap shifting through the forward gear on the other. Drivers no longer had to worry about missing a shift with a manual transmission or knocking it into neutral or reverse with a conventional automatic shifter.

Tempest not only had a 389-cid with Tri Power under the hood, but a Hurst shifter, heavy-duty shocks, and a front roll bar as well.

The result was an easy sell to those at Pontiac, but corporate management at GM would be a hard nut to crack. They had just instituted a corporatewide racing ban on any factory-supported efforts. This was in response to bad press and government concerns about GM's safety record. But the new car was too good of an opportunity to miss, and so DeLorean and Estes found a way

How to tell a real tiger from a pussycat:

Drive it.

Pontiac Motor Division · General Motors Corporation

Two seconds behind the wheel of a Pontiac and you know unquestionably you're in tiger country. You realize right away there's more to being a tiger than just bucket seats, carpeting, and sleek upholstery. There's a six or one of two rambunctious V-8s available in the LeMans. And a snarling 335-hp GTO or its 360-hp cousin. So go drive a tiger!

**Quick Wide-Track Tigers
Pontiac LeMans & GTO**

Opposite bottom: The DeLorean DMC-12 featured a stainless steel body and gull wing doors. This would be the only car that DMC would produce, and only about 8,600 were made between 1981 and 1982, when the company ceased production.

Left: The Wide-Track Tiger campaign advertisements of Jim Wangers are now legendary. Wangers also made TV ads featuring the tiger. During filming in 1966, a tiger became agitated and shredded a car interior while scaring away the crew. Filming resumed twenty minutes later, after the trainer caged the tiger.

All of the performance attributes are touted in this Buick Skylark Gran Sport advertisement. The 400-cid engine packed enough punch to clear the quarter mile in the mid-fifteen-second range. Despite this, about 13,000 Skylarks were produced in 1967.

around the corporate red tape. They would offer the modifications as an optional package rather than as a new production model. Technically, they did not need corporate approval for new options. DeLorean had to decide on a name for his creation and he chose GTO, for Gran Turisimo Omologato, which means Grand Touring Homologated. Homologation specials are officially approved for racing, and this would have a tough and rugged appeal. It had the same European flavor of the existing Le Mans and Grand Prix models. Even the engine displacement was expressed as "6.5 Litre," using the European measurement and spelling.

The production GTO option incorporated the 389-cid with modified 421-cid H.O. heads and Tri Power arrangement producing 348 horsepower. Spent gases exited through a dual-tuned exhaust. The Wide-Track body had heavy-duty springs and shocks, a larger front roll bar with wide rims, and low-profile tires. The standard 3-speed shifter could be replaced with the optional Hurst-Campbell 4-speed for additional cost. Even with all of these performance options, there were those who had doubts about the car's success. Fortunately, advertising man Jim Wangers's aggressive marketing campaign quelled any reservations. The GTO, or "Goat," as it became known, reached production of 32,450 for 1964. Top brass at GM were not happy with Estes or DeLorean, but the additional 40,000 sales the next year silenced any objections. The GTO would go through many changes over the years, including The Judge of 1969–71 and the end-of-the-run Ventura-based GTO of 1974. Nonetheless, the first muscle car had been produced, and the competition would have to scramble to catch up.

The competition included GM divisions that were caught off guard by the Goat. Buick, Chevrolet, and Oldsmobile would soon develop their own muscle cars, even in the face of initial scoffing from corporate headquarters. Buick's answer was to introduce the Gran Sport or GS package to their Skylark of 1965. The Skylark received a 400-cid in V8 with 10.25:1 compression ratio, breathed through dual exhaust and fed through a four-barrel carburetor that produced 325 hp. Power was transmitted to the road via a 2-speed Super Turbine 300 automatic transmission and one of several rear-axle ratios. A reinforced frame, heavy-duty

Superbird.
The Skylark Gran Sport.
400 cu. in. / 325 bhp.
Bucket seats.
Floor-shift, all-synchro 3 speed.
Heavy-duty suspension.
Oversized, 7.75 x 14 tires.
Performance axle ratios.
Zow!
The Buick Skylark
Gran Sport

shocks, springs, and front roll bar kept the car planted to the road. More than 15,000 Skylark buyers chose the GS option that first year.

In 1967, the car was renamed the GS 400 for its all-new 400-cid engine, which replaced the old "nail head" 400. It actually was 401-cid, but GM had placed a maximum 400-cid in engine displacement size on all of its intermediate-bodied cars. The horsepower was increased to 340, and options included a 4-speed manual transmission and a limited-slip differential. Mild cosmetic changes gave way to a more muscular look in 1968. The next year saw further changes, including a cold-air package with a functional hood scoop, pushing the horsepower rating to 345.

The ultimate GS version arrived in 1970 in the form of the GSX, powered by a 455-cid, which produced 350 hp and 510 ft-lbs of torque. In the optional Stage 1 guise, power was increased to 390 hp. A more aggressive camshaft and ignition timing along with specific cylinder heads made this possible. Out of a total production of 678 units, 400 were equipped with the Stage 1 option. This Herculean amount of torque resulted in low- to mid-thirteen-second passes in the quarter-mile dash. A more radical Stage 2 option was offered, but only twelve customers opted for this dealer-installed package. The Stage 2 package was delivered with the parts in the trunk and was meant for off-road use. Initially, only Saturn Yellow and Apollo White were offered as color choices, inspired by the Apollo 11 moon landing the previous year. The next year, the color options expanded to six additional choices. A hood-mounted tachometer kept the driver's eyes on the road.

An optional Stage I package was introduced on the Buick GS 400 in 1969, and it boosted engine ratings to 340 hp and 440 ft-lbs of torque. Fewer than 1,500 Stage I cars were produced in the 1969 model year.

This 1970 Buick GSX is one of only 178 cars produced in Apollo White. Notice that the headlight housings and unique rear spoiler are painted as well.

This hood-mounted tachometer was shared with the Pontiac GTO Judge. Although Pontiac had led the charge with the GTO, Buick had created a winner with the GS, and before either of these, Chevrolet had introduced the Super Sport package to some of their models.

GM's Chevrolet division underwent several changes in 1961. Bunkie Knudsen had made his move from Pontiac to Chevrolet in November of that year. As Chevrolet general manager, he found an ally in Vince Piggins, who had joined Chevrolet in 1956. Piggins had worked his engineering magic on the famous Hudson Hornet before coming to Chevrolet. He would direct most of their performance projects. Chevy had already enjoyed successes at NASCAR since the 1957 season despite an Automobile Manufacturers Association ban on factory racing involvement. The unlikely top-of-the-line Chevy Impala would hit a different kind of track in 1961.

It was that year the Chevy Impala debuted with the Super Sport package and a 409-cid V8. This was derived from the earlier 348-cid power plant. The Impala was a full-sized car, and the muscle of the 409 made it a track star: This newcomer was burning up National Hot Rod Association drag racing events. The engine was only the beginning of the SS package. Exterior trim, spinner hub caps, a heavy-duty suspension, exclusive brakes, and power steering rounded out the package. Super Sport packages would be known as Regular Production Option (RPO) Z03 in 1962–63 and again in 1968.

This unlikely muscle car would undergo many changes. As a full-size car, it originally did not adhere to the usual muscle car formula. Intermediate sedans were still unknown at the time. The Impala SS received a major facelift in 1965. A more curvaceous body resembled the Coke-bottle shape, and the 409-cid engine was available in both 340 hp and 400 hp versions. The ultimate performance engine for the Impala SS would arrive in 1966 in the form of a 427-cid power plant. These so called "Rat" motors could produce 390 or 425 hp and pass the quarter mile in less than sixteen seconds. In 1969, the RPO Z24 would come exclusively with the 427-cid engine. But that marked the final year for the Impala SS, until its return in 1994.

While the Impala filled the full-size category, the all-new A-body Chevelle Malibu would represent the intermediate platform. This effort by

Just starting it makes your stomach muscles tighten

Buckle into that businesslike Corvette seat. Turn the key. Rowrow row . . . BhruUM!

And it happens. The blend of husky, eager noises you expect from a car like the Sting Ray.

That insistent throb is the Turbo-Jet 427 you ordered, 425 horsepower churning under the domed hood.

You sense great gulps of air rushing down through a four-barrel carburetor to their final explosion

while unshrouded valves, solid lifters and a special cam do their stuff.

Now, wipe your perspiring palms and slip that gear box into first cog. Snick! You're about to have a driving experience you'll remember.

Corvette . . . Excitement the Chevrolet Way | CHEVROLET | GM

The 427 Turbo-Jet in the Corvette was shared with the Impala SS of 1966—69. Only 2,124 Impala SS cars were ordered with the RPO Z24 performance package, which included the 427, out of the 1967 total Impala SS production of approximately 76,000.

A blacked-out grill with an SS 396 and double-domed hood are tell-tale signs of the rare Chevelle SS 396 of 1969. The engines in these cars could develop up to 375 hp.

Super Sport option RPO Z15 introduced the 454-cid engine in the Chevelle SS for 1970. In addition to the racing stripes, note the functional hood lock pins, which were part of the additional ZL2 cowl induction hood option.

Chevrolet was to emulate the very popular 1955–57 models in size and concept. The initial 1964 model featured engine options from a lowly 193-cid six to a base 283-cid V8 producing 220 hp. Mid-year models would see the L74 327-cid added to the options list. The Chevelle Super Sport optioned cars received distinguishing trim, interior extras, and the option of a Muncie 4-speed manual or Powerglide automatic transmission. Super Sport models got a big-block boost the next year with a 396-cid V8 as part of the RPO Z16 option package. This would carry over to the 1966 model year in the

new Coke-bottle-styled Chevy Chevelle SS 396 in both sport coupe and convertible bodies.

The following years would see several body changes and additional safety features such as collapsible steering columns and front disc brakes. In 1969, a number of rare Central Office Production Order (COPO) 427-cid engines would be placed in Super Sports. A majority of these would be specially installed by sports car dealer Don Yenko of Canonsburg, Pennsylvania. Seeing this success, the Chevrolet division would release a new 454-cid V8 in 1970. It was available in two versions: the LS5 rated at 360 hp and the LS6 rated at 450 hp. Chevelle Super Sports with these engines represent the best of the breed.

The General Motors A-body would also provide the platform for another muscle car from Oldsmobile. In response to the Pontiac Tempest, the "B09 Police Apprehender" was offered as a mid-year package on the Oldsmobile Cutlass of 1964. A 330-cid V8 rated at 310 hp, 4-barrel carburetor, 4-speed manual transmission, and dual exhaust would bring about the later name of 442. The car was an immediate hit, and many coupes and even a few four-door sedans were produced with the B09 package. The following year, the B09 would be replaced by the F-85 and see the introduction of the 400-cid V8 and the optional 2-speed Jetaway automatic transmission. This was in keeping with the 400-cid limit imposed by GM's top brass. The rare W30 option of 1966 would add the induction of outside air through tubing below the front bumper to the carburetor.

In 1968, the 442 would become its own model, based on the new GM A-body platform. A major restyling would benefit from the performance options offered by George Hurst of Hurst Performance Products. The Hurst/Olds received a 455-cid V8 installed not by GM but by Olds supplier John Demmer. A Hurst Dual-Gate shifter would be standard, and a

Fewer than fifty Oldsmobile 442 Holiday Sport Coupes were optioned with the 5A trim package as seen here. A 400-cid V8 and Jetaway automatic transmission power this rare 442.

Forced-Air Induction was available on the mid-level Cutlass S model. This advertisement highlights the performance options for the younger generation of Oldsmobile buyers.

What are those funny things under the bumper?

Olds Cutlass S

distinguishing silver and black trim identified the car. The paint scheme would change to gold and white on the next model year. John Beltz, who was the engineer on both the Toronado and 442 projects, was promoted to Oldsmobile general manager in 1969, a post he would hold until his early death at age forty-six in 1972. Beltz was an industry visionary who saw the 442 evolve until its final year as a separate series in 1971.

The folks at Ford Motor Company would enter the muscle car competition with their own full-size and intermediate models. Some of the models, such as Galaxie and Fairlane, had been around since the 1950s. New performance and aggressive restyling would turn these family movers into street machines.

The Ford Galaxie 500 XL combined performance and comfort in a full-size car. Rear leaf springs were replaced, and the Galaxie got coil springs all around for 1965.

The Ford Galaxie was a full-size competitor to the Chevy Impala. First released in 1959, the 1961 model had new styling and a more powerful 390-cid V8 available in two forms, a four-barrel or three two-barrel versions. This offered up to 401 hp, which moved this full-size car in fast luxury. Displacement would increase again the next year with the 406-cid V8 offered over the base 292-cid V8. The Galaxie 500 XL of 1962 was offered in response to the Super Sport option on Chevy's Impala. This was available in either two-door hardtop or convertible form. A "Sports Roof" or fastback model would be offered the next year. A new model arrived in 1966 called

HOW TO COOK A TIGER

Take one part 335 HP V-8. Chrome plate the rocker covers, oil filler cap, radiator cap, air cleaner cover and dip stick.

Blend high lift cam; bigger carburetor.

Mix in the new 2-way, 3-speed GTA Sport Shift that you can use either manually or let shift itself.

Place the new shift selector between great bucket seats.

Now put on competition type springs and shocks.

Add a heavy-duty stabilizer bar.

Place over low profile 7.75 nylon whitewalls.

Touch off with distinctive GTA medallion and contrasting racing stripe.

Cover with hardtop or 5-ply vinyl convertible top with glass rear window. Serve in any of 15 colors.

This is the new Fairlane GTA. An original Ford recipe that may be tasted at your Ford Dealers . . . Remember--it's a very hot dish!

FAIRLANE

GTA

A PRODUCT OF Ford

This Ford Fairlane GTA advertisement takes a shot at the competition without mentioning them by name. The Fairlane depicted seems to have devoured a tiger from one of the Pontiac Tiger ads of the time.

the Galaxie 500 7 Litre. This model boasted a new 428-cid Thunderbird V8. The new coil sprung suspension was carried over from the previous year. Interior padding, an energy-absorbing steering column, and a dual-brake cylinder were just a few of the safety features that would be expanded upon. The Galaxie itself would soldier on until 1974 with reduced horsepower, though after 1969 as a less-than-muscular figure.

The Ford Fairlane was moved into the intermediate category in 1962, but it did not receive muscle car status until 1966, when the GT and GTA packages were introduced for the Fairlane 500. Most Fairlanes were hardtops, but the rare convertible was available. The GT received the 390-cid V8 producing 335 hp, and the GTA received a SportShift Cruise-O-Matic automatic transmission. A small number of Fairlane 500s were equipped with a 427-cid engine that produced 425 hp. Those who opted for the GT were rewarded with a special hood and body stripes in addition to power disc brakes and Wide-Oval tires. These cars were popular on both the road and track. The top performance engines came in 1968 with the 428-cid Cobra-Jet and Super Cobra-Jet. The model also received a redesign and the introduction of a "Sports Roof" or fastback body. This was also the year that the GTs became part of the Torino range.

The Torino began life as an upscale version of the Fairlane but would become Ford's primary intermediate offering. With the Fairlane reduced to being a base model Torino, the Torino GT would carry performance forward

Henry Ford II devoted great effort to beat Enzo Ferrari on European race tracks after Ferrari broke off negotiations to sell his company to Ford. The result was the Ford GT40, which won four consecutive times at Le Mans.

Anyone can paint stripes on a car...we earned ours at Le Mans...Sebring... Indianapolis...

When you go fastback or GT... you've got to go Ford! And one of the reasons why is the newest member of Ford's winning fastback pack, the Torino GT. Built on a 116-inch wheelbase, this one sports such standard equipment items as a 302-cu. in. V-8, SelectShift transmission, unique GT stripes and identification, styled steel wheels and wide-oval tires.

But, Ford didn't stop with one well-bred fastback, it went on to make an entire pack . . . five models in three different sizes . . . small, medium, and large. Ford calls them the Mustang Fastback 2+2, Torino GT fastback, Fairlane 500 fastback, Ford XL fastback and Ford Galaxie 500 fastback. People who consider driving a sport a call them great. The reasons why are as varied as the selection of models and options.

Consider five different V-8's for the XL. These run all the way from a new 302-cu. in. jewel with special light-weight pistons, to the proven 428-cu. in. V-8. These range from 210 to 360 hp. With five V-8's each for Torino, Fairlane and Mustang, the fastback pack really lays on the V-8 choice.

They're not stinting on transmissions either. On most of these engines you can have either 3-speed, 4-speed, or syrup-smooth 3-range SelectShift. That's the automatic that leaves the option to shift or not to shift up to you. Ford doesn't let you build in all this go without having something special in the stop department. That something is a new optional floating-caliper disc brake that quickly disperses heat for high fade resistance, more uniform braking action.

There are eight V-8's, three transmissions, two suspensions, three tire options, two brake setups and five models . . . if your choice is GT or fastback, is there any doubt that Ford gives you the biggest choice? There's no need to choose things like stripes, low-restriction exhaust, and special wheel covers . . . Ford includes these in the special GT packages available for both Ford and Mustang.

If there's a fastback in this mix with your name on it, the nicest surprise is yet to come. Just because it's pretty doesn't mean that Ford is going to twist your arm. You'll see what we mean when you check the price tag. Get the message? Ford did . . . loud and clear.

FORD ...has a better idea.

in 1969. The Torino GT also featured the 428-cid Cobra-Jet, and a new Ram Air induction package was optional. As with many of the cars from this era, corresponding emblems would adorn the fenders to advertise engine displacement. The 428-4V Super Cobra-Jet became the top performance engine offered for 1969. This engine was designed with drag racing in mind and was referred to as being part of the "Drag-Pack" option. Special rear axle gears and a Traction-Lock differential helped put the power to the ground. A new, more pronounced Coke-bottle body would be introduced in 1970, along with the optional 429-cid V8. The Torino Cobra would produce 370 hp with this engine, which was carried over into the next year. A blacked-out hood, 7-inch-wide wheels shod with Wide-Oval tires, and a competition suspension would make 1971 a great year for the Torino.

The new fastback design of 1968 greatly out-sold the notch back version of the Comet. Those few Cyclones equipped with the 427 engine are greatly sought after today by collectors.

The restyled 1970 Mercury Cyclone was not to everyone's taste. A base Cyclone Spoiler was loaded for battle, though with many performance upgrades and the formidable 429 CJ V8.

Although the Torino would remain until 1976, the models after 1971 were more refined and less powerful.

The Ford Fairlane was the basis for another model that did not share Ford's "Blue Oval" but was a "messenger of the gods." The heavens would certainly be the place to look for inspiration in naming Mercury automobiles. The Mercury Comet Cyclone and later GT is such a car. Originally a compact car, it grew in size to become an intermediate-class contender. The GT model of 1966 would boast power in the form of a 390-cid V8 producing 335 hp. This engine would continue to be the top performer until the arrival of the 428 CJ and briefly the 427-cid V8s of 1968. Several safety features appeared as well. Dual brakes and an energy-absorbing steering column were new features. It was also the last year for the hardtop; only the fastback would continue.

By 1970, the top contender was the 429 SCJ Cyclone Spoiler. With 375 hp on tap and a unique gun sight grill, this machine was ready for action. The availability of psychedelic colors and graphics made this car stand out among more pedestrian transportation. Despite all the positive press, however, sales on the Cyclone were far below the Torino. But competition came not only from within.

It was originally the Dodge Brothers, John and Horace, who supplied Henry Ford with Model T components before they launched their own automotive company in November 1914. They began supplying engines,

Dodge Rebellion fever was in full bloom in 1966 with the new fastback Charger. A powerful punch could be delivered by the new 426 street Hemi, purpose-built for street use. Only 468 of more than 37,000 Chargers had this option.

Only 207 Charger R/T cars would be equipped with both the Hemi and a manual 4-speed transmission in 1969. The F8 Brilliant Dark Green Metallic paint also makes this Charger stand out from the crowd.

transmissions, and axles to Ford in 1903. The first Dodge Brothers car, the Dodge Four, was a far cry from the later Dodge and other Chrysler Motor Corporation muscle cars. The Dodge Charger and Coronet R/T would emulate the volatile personality of the older brother John Dodge.

It was 1966 when executives at Dodge decided to present the Dodge Charger to head the "Dodge Rebellion." Labeled as a sports sedan, it was actually a streamlined Coronet with fastback styling. A base 318-cid V8 or optional 383-cid V8 would propel this rebel. The 426-cid Hemi was offered as an option, along with a TorqueFlite automatic transmission or a 4-speed manual. A Hemi-powered Charger could pass the quarter mile in the mid-fourteen-second range in sporty room and comfort. Hemi-powered cars are rare: Only 118 were built out of 15,788 total Chargers in 1967.

This Charger Super Bee of 1971 is in Top Banana paint and features a V code 440 V8 with a Six-Pack and a 4-speed manual transmission. Only thirty cars were produced with this power train combination.

The 1968 GTX.
The idle alone sounds like the William Tell Overture.

It goes "Rumpety-Rumpety-Rumpety-Rumpety-Rumpety-Rumpety-Rumpety..."
The reason for that is the high-lift, long-duration cam which nestles amid GTX's 440 cu. in., 375 hp V-8.
You turn it on. And it reciprocates.
And the beat goes on.

We figure a Supercar should look the part, too. *Form follows function,* and all that.
So this year we gave GTX a completely new body.
Note the new hood, grille, fenders, roofline, Wide Boots—everything.
And the beat goes on.

Inside, there's a new instrument panel and simulated wood accents everywhere you look.
If you order a tach, you'll find it mounted right near the speedometer.
And if you so specify, we'll connect it to our famed 426 Street Hemi.
It goes "Rumpety-Rump," also.
And the beat goes on.

Plymouth

CHRYSLER
MOTORS CORPORATION

...the Plymouth win-you-over beat goes on

The first Charger R/T of 1968 featured new Coke-bottle styling, bumble-bee stripes around the rear of the car, dual exhaust, and a handling package. A high compression 440-cid Magnum V8 would power the R/T, and the Hemi would be an option. The R/T meant that the car could be driven on the road or raced on a track. The Charger would receive a complete restyling in 1971 and feature a standard 383-cid V8. Super Bees received the 440-cid with the "Six Pack" sporting 390 hp or the optional 426-cid Hemi producing 485 hp. The Six Pack consists of three two-barrel carburetors, which provide more fuel and air to the engine resulting in more horsepower. These cars are very rare, with only twenty-two Charger Super Bees built with the Hemi option. The high-performance Charger would end in 1971, replaced with a less powerful but more luxurious package.

The Plymouth Belvedere GTX and Road Runner shared the Chrysler B-body platform with the Dodge Charger but offered their own brand of excitement. The GTX offered a balance of luxury and performance, while the Road Runner was a more stripped-down version of the GTX. The Road Runner was intended for the youth market, hence the use of Warner Brothers's famous cartoon character in both name and likeness. Even the horn sounded the famous cartoon bird's "beep-beep" to other motorists. The omission of insulation, roof vinyl, and trim, and a Spartan interior helped to reduce weight and quarter-mile times. It was introduced with a 383-cid V8, 4-speed transmission, and heavy-duty suspension as standard; an optional 426 Hemi also was available. Styling changes and new options made 1969 a stellar year. The optional 440 Six Pack was introduced with the additional "Air Grabber" hood and a Hurst shifter. High Impact colors would be offered the next year to stand out on the street or track. The Road Runner was produced as a coupe, hardtop, and convertible until 1971.

The full-size and intermediate muscle cars represented a generational change to the American automotive industry. Pontiac's GTO would be the impetus for an American automotive revolution followed by other manufacturers. Many designers and engineers would struggle against corporate bureaucracy to see their dreams realized. Another car would launch a whole new type of muscle car called the pony.

Opposite: The Plymouth Belvedere GTX featured vents on the hood, which could be manually opened to provide fresh intake air and additional power to the standard 440 engine under the hood.

Warner Brothers received $50,000 for the use of their famous cartoon character. The car featured a beep-beep horn just like its namesake, which cost an additional $10,000 to develop.

Sally and Dennis Koelmel's idea of a weekend drive in the country.

Of course they use such special equipment as a time/distance calculator, driving lights, a rally odometer, etc. But that's all that distinguishes Sally and Dennis Koelmel's rally 'Cuda from one you might buy yourself. As a matter of fact, Dennis and Sally use theirs throughout the week for such varied ends as commuting, grocery shopping and skiing trips. It's *that* kind of car.

Barracuda's handling, for example, enables it to squirt through town as easily as it takes an S-turn in the country. Especially if it has the optional Formula S suspension and quick-steering ratio, like the Koelmel's.

Then there's reliability. Car-busting roads don't faze the 'Cuda one flap. It starts in the morning, too. And to our knowledge, no one ever won a rally or got to work on time stranded in some out-of-the-way garage.

Comfort? There's room enough inside for legs, instruments, friends, the navigator—even stranded competitors.

But even if rallying isn't your idea of a weekend drive in the country, Barracuda's your kind of machine.

Personally, we can't imagine a sportier way to bring home a couple of bags of cement. Barracuda, as you can plainly see, is out to win you over. **'67 Barracuda.**

3-time SCCA National Rally Champions, Sally and Dennis Koelmel.

Plymouth   CHRYSLER MOTORS CORPORATION

PONY STAMPEDE

O N APRIL 17, 1964, a new white convertible with red interior was introduced at the New York City World's Fair that would take America by storm. Millions visiting the fair would see the new Ford Mustang, named after the famous World War II American P-51 fighter plane. This affordable, sporty car with a galloping horse on the grill would enable Ford to sell more than 22,000 initial units. By the end of the first year, more than 400,000 Ford Mustangs had been sold. Thus was the thunderous beginning of the pony car.

The Mustang story began a few years earlier as the vision of Lee Iacocca. Iacocca had been with Ford since the 1950s. He envisioned a fun-to-drive, compact car with sporting performance for young buyers. He received approval and funding to move forward with the project in September 1962. Ford Chief Engineer Donald Frey would conceive the first prototype that same year. After several changes, Project Design Chief Joe Oros and his team would create the first clay model of the eventual 1964½ production Mustang. Many of the components for the Mustang would be borrowed from the existing Ford Falcon. This reduced cost and expedited production.

"The car to be designed by you" marketing slogan applied to the first and many of the following Mustangs. A wide range of options appealed to men and women alike. After all, about half of the Mustangs sold were purchased by women. Some ordered the base model with a 170-cid 6-cylinder and 3-speed manual transmission. Daring individuals would desire the 289-cid V8 with a 4-speed manual transmission. The manual transmissions were floor shifts, but an optional automatic transmission also was available.

The 1965 model year saw the addition of the 2+2 fastback body to expand on the coupe and convertible offerings. Other additions were the décor group that introduced what was known as the "Pony Interior," a GT equipment group that offered better instrumentation, dual exhaust, a quicker steering ratio, performance brakes, sway bars, and grill-mounted fog lights. The interior color and style choices would increase again the next year to offer thirty-four varieties.

Opposite:
The Plymouth Barracuda S made its reputation on great handling that the Koelmels put to good use. Rallying presented many challenges as a variety of road surfaces and environments tested the performance of any car. Rally winners were frequently used in advertising campaigns that promoted endurance and performance.

Above: Carroll Shelby was a race car driver turned tuner and manufacturer of high-performance cars. His involvement in the Ford GT40 program and later AC Cobras is well known. Shelby was approached by Lee Iacocca to help produce limited-edition Mustangs offering higher performance. The Shelby GT350 and 500 are rare and desirable cars today.

Right: Lee Iacocca is seen here in 1993 with President Bill Clinton, a Mustang owner and enthusiast. Iacocca's political influence paid off for Chrysler when he secured a loan guarantee from the U.S. government in 1979, which saved the company from bankruptcy.

Right: This ad encourages readers to visit the Ford Motor Company's Rotunda at the 1964 New York World's Fair and to see the new Mustang. The Mustang was a sporty and economical car that was to be "designed by you."

Presenting
the unexpected...
new Ford Mustang!
$2368* f.o.b. Detroit

FORD

The Mustang
interior was
smartly appointed
for its price.
The driver and
passengers are
reminded of what
kind of car they
are in by the
running pony logo.

A major restyling would arrive in 1967 with the first opportunity to
boost performance with a big block. In addition to a wider body for better
handling, a 390-cid V8 was optional. This big block power could be controlled
with the new FMX transmission and power disc brakes. Novelties such as
AM/FM stereo and a rear defogger would not arrive until the next model
year. U.S. Government safety regulations would make themselves known
through side marker lights and an energy-absorbing steering column.

1968 was the
last year for the
fastback style,
which would be
replaced by a
Sports Roof
design. The
fastback Mustang
GT remains one
of the more
collectable regular
production models
today.

This performance market engine was launched in 1968 and rated at 335 hp, but in actuality produced closer to 410 hp. The under rating of this engine illustrates the growing concerns over insurance premiums.

"Hot Rod" Sees the Light

"The Cobra Jet will be the utter delight of every Ford lover and the bane of all the rest because, quite frankly, it is the fastest running Pure Stock in the history of man."

HOT ROD MAGAZINE
March, 1968

Ford introduces the 428-cu. in. Cobra Jet V-8

See the light—the switch is on to Ford!

One good bit of news was the replacement of the 289-cid V8 with the new 302-cid V8, which could produce 210 to 230 hp.

Exciting new models in 1969 would become legendary in the muscle car arena. The most obvious change was the departure of the 2+2 fastback styling in favor of a Sportsroof design. A 351-cid V8 would be one of five larger engines available. The even larger 428-cid Cobra Jet could command 335 hp on request. But the most recognizable of the new models has to be the

Only 2,539 Mach 1s were built in Bright Gold Metallic. This 1970 R code model features a 428 Cobra Jet V8 and a close ratio 4-speed manual transmission and the rare option of a factory-installed tachometer.

Mustang Mach 1. A low-gloss black hood with a hood scoop made this model stand out. Limited production runs of this model included the Boss 302 and Boss 429. These racing-inspired cars produced 290 hp and 375 hp, respectively. The Boss 302 was designed to meet Sports Car Club of America (SCCA) Trans-Am rules, and the Boss 429 was a homologation special for NASCAR. The trunk-mounted battery and flared fenders, to accommodate the Magnum 500 chrome wheels, are a testimony to its racing pedigree. These models would remain in production until 1971.

As with each major styling before, the 1971 Mustangs grew in both size and weight. Designer Larry Shinoda was influential in the distinct Kamm rear-end styling and is revered for the Boss 302 project and earlier work with GM on the Corvette. It would also be the last year for the big block. The Boss 351 was replacing the 302, and the Boss 429 remained with the option of Ram Air. These packages would be dropped the next year with the sole performance model being the Mach 1 with a low-compression 351 H.O. V8. The last of the big Mustangs would be in 1973, and it would be a decade before a convertible would be offered again.

Just as Iacocca had begun to move forward with the Mustang project in 1962, Chevrolet Chief Designer Irv Rybicki had his own idea for a pony car. It was then that Rybicki first presented his Chevy II-based "Super Nova" concept to GM Styling Vice President Bill Mitchell. Mitchell liked the idea and shared it with then Chevrolet General Manager Bunkie Knudsen. Knudsen was concerned about introducing another vehicle line where five already existed, if the upcoming Chevelle was included. Reluctantly, Knudsen presented the idea to GM President Jack Gordon and corporate management. The conservative management team rejected the idea and thought that the Corvair could be competitive with any rival offerings. Despite this setback, Hank Haga, chief of Chevrolet's Studio Three, would continue to work on concepts with Assistant Studio Chief John Schinella.

When introduced, the Chevelle was available in seven different body styles. The Chevelle Malibu SS convertible portrayed here was a rare sight in 1964 and is highly sought after today.

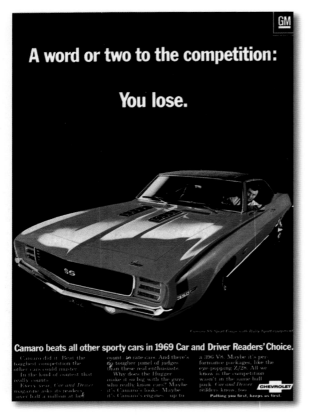

A word or two to the competition:

You lose.

Camaro SS Sport Coupe with Rally Sport equipment

Camaro beats all other sporty cars in 1969 Car and Driver Readers' Choice.

Camaro did it. Beat the toughest competition the other cars could muster. In the kind of contest that really counts.

Every year, *Car and Driver* magazine asks its readers, over half a million at last count, to rate cars. And there's no tougher panel of judges than these real enthusiasts.

Why does the Hugger make it so big with the guys who really know cars? Maybe it's Camaro's looks. Maybe it's Camaro's engines – up to

a 396 V8. Maybe it's performance packages, like the eye-popping Z/28. All we know is the competition wasn't in the same ball park. *Car and Driver* readers know, too.

Putting you first, keeps us first.

CHEVROLET

The best of both worlds is embodied in this Camaro Super Sport with the Rally Sport package. Although a 396 was an optional engine, this Camaro advertised on each front fender that it had a 350 under the hood. Notice the covered headlights, which are part of the RS equipment.

Finally, in August 1964, GM corporate management approved the project. It was codenamed XP-836 and based on the Chevy II to reduce costs. This codename would give way to the name Panther and then Camaro. Camaro had a French definition of "comrade" or "pal," which fit with the tailored-by-owner concept. The folks at Ford had a bit of fun when they found a Spanish definition meaning "shrimp." The laughter was short lived, however, when the Camaro was launched on schedule in September 1966.

The new F-body platform would be the basis for the Camaro in either a coupe or convertible, which incorporated 2+2 seating. A straight-six or five V8 engines were available with either a 3- or 4-speed manual or Powerglide transmission. Distinct Rally Sport and Super Sport options were available. The desirable appearance Rally Sport option package featured pivoting headlight covers and a "bumble bee" stripe around the nose of the car. This was inspired by fighter planes, reducing glare against the canopy and visually shortening the nose. The Super Sport option boasted a domed hood, performance suspension, and the new 350-cid V8. The largest V8 option would be the RPO L34 396-cid big block. Piggins had helped to create a powerful 302-cid V8 for the Camaro Z/28. This special model was created for use in the SCCA Trans-Am series, and their displacement cap was 305 cid. Camaro made another immediate splash into racing by providing RS/SS convertibles as pace cars for the 1967 Indianapolis 500.

The rarest of Camaros would follow in 1969 with the Central Office Production Order (COPO) 8008, Yenko Camaro. These cars had factory-installed L72 427-cid V8 engines ordered by Yenko. Fred Gibb and Beger Chevrolet dealers would also order COPO units as well. Production numbered around 200 of these special cars. Fred Gibb also approached Piggins about the construction of a National Hot Rod Association (NHRA) qualifying Camaro. Piggins conferred with Chevrolet General Manager Pete Estes, who said that if fifty were purchased, they would build them. Gibb accepted, and the ZL-1 Camaro became a reality. This included the coveted aluminum 427-cid V8. Although fifty were purchased by Gibb, an additional nineteen went to other dealers. Drag racer Dickie Harrell registered a best performance in the quarter mile of just over ten seconds at 139 mph driving one of these cars. Therein lies the great strength and flexibility of the COPO program.

A late arrival for 1970 was the second-generation Camaro. A complete restyling featured a semifastback roofline; no convertible was offered. The base V8 was the 307-cid engine. In addition, the RPO Z27 SS option had a 350-cid V8, and the SS 396 option had a 402-cid engine. The Z/28 was still offered in coupe form only. Major changes would take place over the next couple of years, and trouble loomed on the horizon. Horsepower ratings

dropped in 1971, and the LT-1 396-cid V8 was only producing 240 net horsepower. The Camaro model almost did not survive past the 1972 model year. Labor disputes resulted in a 174-day long strike at the Norwood Assembly Plant in Ohio, the main plant for assembling Camaros. Large numbers of partially completed cars were scrapped rather than trying to upgrade them to meet ever more stringent 1973 standards. GM executives then thought about ending the Camaro for good. Chevrolet Engineering Director Alexander C. Mair fought for the survival of the Camaro and is credited as its savior. Mair personally appealed to top brass at GM and promised the Camaro was worth the investment. Thankfully, the GM executives relented and the Camaro would endure, although with breaks in production, until today.

The GM F-body would provide the platform of another long-lasting American icon, the Pontiac Firebird. Introduced in the same year as the Camaro, the Firebird had its own distinguishing elements. A divided front

The 1969 Z/28 is one of the most iconic Camaros ever. It may only have had a 302-cid V8, but this engine was meant more for the racetrack than for drag races. Peak horsepower and torque were at 5,800 and 4,200 rpm, respectively.

Second-generation
Camaros were
produced until
1981. The
Norwood Plant
strike of 1972 may
well have made
this the last
generation of
Camaros.

grill and integral bumper were obvious departures from its Camaro cousin. The most potent model, the Firebird 400, would include Pontiac's own 400-cid V8 producing 325 hp. Chrome engine accents and a dual exhaust system with Ram Air option contributed to making the Firebird 400 a looker and performer in either a coupe or convertible form.

The Firebird 400 was a powerful and popular model, spawning several variants. Halfway through 1969, the SCCA sedan racing Firebird Trans Am would compete in its own cup series. Only twenty-five were actually made for the series, but a production model would follow. By mid-1970, four models were available in hard top form: Firebird, Espirit, Formula 400, and the Trans Am. The top engine available was the 400-cid with Ram Air IV, which produced 370 hp. This would be improved upon the next year by the introduction of the 455-cid V8. Two versions of the 455 were offered over the base 350- and 400-cid engines. A standard 455-cid V8 would produce 325 hp, and the 455 H.O. or "high output" would produce 335 hp. The 455 H.O. engine would replace the 400 due to lower compression ratios and horsepower reductions. Production of all 1972 models was affected by the same UAW strike at the Norwood, Ohio, plant that almost ended the Camaro. Despite this, the Firebird rose like a phoenix and survived this near catastrophe. However, the sun was setting on the muscle car era. The last muscle bound Firebirds, a Formula and Trans Am, with an SD or "super duty" 455-cid V8, produced only 250 hp in 1974.

It's hard to believe that just ten years earlier the Ford Mustang charged onto the muscle car scene and quickly stole the show from yet another pony car from Plymouth. The Plymouth Barracuda was the creation of General Manager P. N. Buckminster, who wanted to build a car for young, sports-minded Americans. It was also in part a reaction to the Ford Falcon, upcoming Mustang, and the Chevrolet Corvair Monza. It is correct to say "upcoming" concerning the Mustang because the Barracuda was released about two weeks earlier. Using the existing Plymouth Valiant and giving it a fastback roofline helped to quicken its ultimate production in 1964. Initially, a choice of three engines could be coupled to one of two manual transmissions or the TorqueFlite automatic.

Exciting news arrived in 1965 for Barracuda fans. An improved "Golden Commando" version of the 273-cid V8 was offered as part of the "S" package, which included a heavy-duty suspension. Minor changes to the Golden Commando would occur the next year for participation in the SCCA National Rally Class. The 1967 model year saw the introduction of a 280 hp 383-cid V8 big-block offering. This was accompanied by minor styling changes and the introduction of the notchback and convertible. George Hurst would work his magic on the Barracuda in 1968 with the resulting "Hurst Hemi." This car featured the 426-cid Street Hemi and was intended for use in NHRA Super Stock drag racing events. An estimated fifty of these cars were built utilizing lightweight materials such as fiberglass fenders and Chemcor side glass.

Performance upgrades were bound for street Barracudas in 1969. A replacement for the S option was the shortened 'Cuda trim package. This would cause all high-performance models to be marketed as the shortened 'Cuda. Power plants consisted of a 340-, 383-, and the new 440-cid Super Commando V8. A total redesign in 1970 finally broke any

400 badges on the hood of this Firebird give it away. The Ram Air option could boost engine output up to 370 hp. A rare dealer-installed Ram Air V could bring the power up to 500 hp.

1974 Pontiac Firebirds.

Part engineering.
Part soul.

There's something about a 1974 Firebird you won't find in any fact sheet or spec book.

Because it's something you can't weigh or measure or touch. It's something you have to feel.

We call it soul.

Take the '74 Formula Firebird for example. Any spec sheet will tell you it comes with a 350, 400 or 455 V-8. A floor-shifted 3-speed

trans. Performance dual exhausts. Hood scoops. Front disc brakes. And front and rear stabilizers. A very impressive list of features.

But no feature list can explain what it's like to drive a Formula Bird. Gauges set so you can read them at a glance. Controls positioned so they seem like they're extensions of your arms and legs. Response so quick it almost anticipates your commands. And an overall driving

experience that makes it hard to suppress a toothy grin.

That's the soul of a Firebird.

The '74 Firebird Trans Am is even better. Because what we know about performance driving, we make standard on Trans Am.

A 400 4-bbl. V-8. 4-speed trans. Power front disc brakes. A limited-slip axle. Full instrumentation. F60 – 15 tires on 7" Rally II wheels.

A shaker hood. A complete entourage of functional air dams, extractors, deflectors and spoilers.

And enough soul to make Trans Am the ultimate Firebird.

Anybody can appreciate Firebird's engineering. To appreciate its soul, you have to love driving cars. As much as we love building them.

The Wide-Track people have a way with cars.

The 1974 SD 455-equipped Firebird Trans Am was the last of the real muscle cars produced. Clear in this image is the shaker hood on the red Trans Am.

Opposite:
A seventh engine was available as a drag race only Super Stock 426 Hemi package. These cars are extremely rare, with only fifty produced. They were not to be used on public highways and could run mid-ten-second quarter-mile times.

commonality with the Valiant. The fastback styling gave way to either a hard two-door top or a convertible. The 426 Hemi was now available for the street with a larger engine bay from the redesign. A standard 383-cid V8 was more than adequate producing 355 hp, but discerning buyers could opt for the Hemi producing 425 hp. The Hemi's two four-barreled carburetors breathed through an Air Grabber or "shaker" hood scoop. The scoop was mounted to the engine and would thus move or shake with engine vibrations.

An amazing choice of seven engines was available in hardtop and convertible 'Cudas in 1971. The top options would be the 440-cid "Six-Pack" or the 426 Hemi. These produced 385 hp and 425 hp, respectively. Special decals and dazzling colors made these cars stand out. This was the last great year for the 'Cuda. By 1972, the base engine was the 318-cid V8, and the only other V8 offered was a 340.

Outside of the Big Three, there was a younger company who wanted to change their conservative image with a competitive pony car of their own. American Motors Corporation was formed in 1954 by the merging of Nash-Kelvinator Corporation and the Hudson Motor Car Company. Nash and Hudson were both familiar brands in the automotive world that would be phased out by 1957. The famous AMC Rambler would be the initial offering that embodied the economical approach of the company.

The 1968 Barracuda.
We gave it 4 new engines,
just for kicks.

We widened Barracuda's optional Wide Oval tires.
And blended the taillights with the rear deck.
And restyled the grille.
In short, we made it look a whole lot cleaner and quicker.
And the beat goes on.

We also gave Barracuda options it never had before.
Like carpeting on the walls.
And map pouches on the doors.
Order a tach and you'll find the shift points in the "12 o'clock" position.
They're easier to see that way.
And the beat goes on.

Our new engines: 318, 340 and 383 cu. in. V-8s and a 225 cu. in. Six.
Powering your choice of hardtop, fastback or convertible body styles.
And the beat goes on.

Plymouth

CHRYSLER
MOTORS CORPORATION

...the Plymouth win-you-over beat goes on

AMC heavily advertised their racing success. The reputation of the AMX and Javelin were born on the race track. Here we see the points made from record-breaking endurance and speed events in 1968.

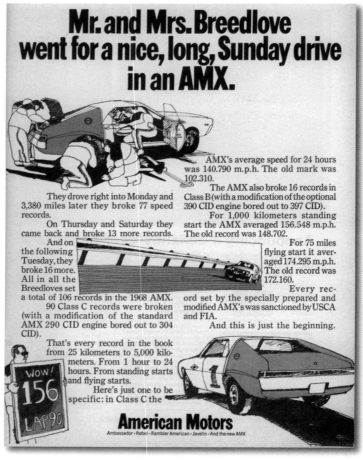

Mr. and Mrs. Breedlove went for a nice, long, Sunday drive in an AMX.

They drove right into Monday and 3,380 miles later they broke 77 speed records.

On Thursday and Saturday they came back and broke 13 more records. And on the following Tuesday, they broke 16 more. All in all the Breedloves set a total of 106 records in the 1968 AMX.

90 Class C records were broken (with a modification of the standard AMX 290 CID engine bored out to 304 CID).

That's every record in the book from 25 kilometers to 5,000 kilometers. From 1 hour to 24 hours. From standing starts and flying starts.

Here's just one to be specific: in Class C the

AMX's average speed for 24 hours was 140.790 m.p.h. The old mark was 102.310.

The AMX also broke 16 records in Class B (with a modification of the optional 390 CID engine bored out to 397 CID).

For 1,000 kilometers standing start the AMX averaged 156.548 m.p.h. The old record was 148.702.

For 75 miles flying start it averaged 174.295 m.p.h. The old record was 172.160.

Every record set by the specially prepared and modified AMX's was sanctioned by USCA and FIA.

And this is just the beginning.

WOW! 156 LAP 90

American Motors

Ambassador · Rebel · Rambler American · Javelin · And the new AMX

AMC typically abstained from the usual yearly makeovers of their competitors. As a result their models became stagnant, and sales along with shares suffered. It was during this time, in early 1967, that Roy D. Chapin, Jr. was appointed CEO of AMC. Chapin instituted many changes that cut costs and provided customers with more value for a lower sticker price. One example is that AMC was the first U.S. automaker to make air conditioning standard equipment on a line of cars. Changing the image of AMC to one that appealed to the youth market with sporty attributes was Chapin's goal. It happened that AMC had two models in development embodying this idea.

The AMC Javelin and AMX were both developed simultaneously with full scale models being conceived in 1965. Chairman of the Board of

Directors Robert B. Evans pushed for a more sporty offering in the AMC lineup and wanted to see the cars put quickly into production. Unfortunately for Evans, it would be Chapin who would preside over the cars' release after Evans resigned as chairman and CEO predecessor Roy Abernathy was forced out over the slump in sales.

The Javelin and AMX are not your typical pony cars. Although the Javelin was a four-seater, the AMX or American Motors Experimental was a two-seater. The Coke-bottle styling transformed to a very short wheelbase with a very small rear deck and a long hood. The car handled extremely well and had muscle to boot. Many automotive writers at the time said that the AMX acted like both a sports car and a muscle car. The 390-cid engine produced 315 hp and the heavy-duty suspension provided nimble handling. The model would see changes over its four-year lifespan. The "Big Bad" option of 1969 incorporated neon-colored body paint. Functional ram-air induction was part of the "Go Package" from 1970. A restyling and standard 360-cid V8 appeared for the 1970 model year. This would be the last year for the AMX as a two-seater. The Javelin body would be shared by both cars until the end came in 1974.

The engine bay of an AMX filled with its 390-cid V8. This engine shared components and machining with AMC's 290 and 343 engines for economical manufacturing purposes.

Scott Harvey's family car.

Some family car! Scott's car, like most of those campaigned in serious sedan racing, has been specially modified to make it a little more race car and a little less street machine.

It's sort of interesting to note, though, that there are several things that didn't need changing to turn our Formula 'S' Barracuda into a SCCA National Champion. Like disc brakes. And the heavy-duty suspension. And the limited-slip differential. And the basics of our 273-cu.-in. V-8. And the fast-ratio steering gear . . . all of these standard or available on the production Formula 'S'.

And so are a few other items that make the 'S' a car that's perfect for the street, and that can still knock off an occasional rally or gymkhana. Front bucket seats, a rear seat that flips down into a seven-foot-long cargo space and slippery fastback styling.

Now with all of this, don't you think it might be more fun to win a rally with a family car? Talk to your Plymouth Dealer right away and see.

PLYMOUTH DIVISION ★ **CHRYSLER** MOTORS CORPORATION

Plymouth ...a great car by Chrysler Corporation.

TRACK TIME

Since the dawn of the automobile, man has been obsessed with making cars go faster and pitting models against one another. Individuals and manufacturers have found great rewards in motor sport. Racing is the ultimate test of durability and reliability of a specific model or design. It is also a constant research and development effort to improve performance and safety features that often find their way into production models. Individuals and manufacturers have found motor sport competition to be a useful tool. Some could prove the reliability of a design through endurance events and others pit different makes against one another. It stands to reason that any performance car or muscle car would be a natural in many forms of motor sport.

Certain muscle cars were homologation specials purposely built for racing in specifically sanctioned events. These specials were built as a requirement for a particular model to enter competition. Most sanctioning bodies required that the car be available to the public and that a certain minimum number be produced. The National Hot Rod Association, National Association for Stock Car Auto Racing, and Sports Car Club of America all saw major participation by muscle cars, if not outright domination. The origins of these sanctioning bodies began just before and during World War II.

Originally known as the bad-boy sport, drag racing advanced from the streets to organized events held by the NHRA. Even before the formation of the NHRA, many early drag racers would race against the clock, usually in a quarter-mile dash, in their modified Ford Model T or Model A. The hot modification was to shoehorn the famous flat-head Ford V8 into the Model Ts and Model As and cut away the fenders for reduced weight. It was during the pre-World War II period that pairs of cars began to make acceleration runs against one another in the quarter mile. Such races continued after World War II, when many former American servicemen were able to use their newfound knowledge in machinery and metallurgy toward preparing drag cars. Unfortunately, the street racing also continued, and casualties

Opposite: Although rally driver Scott Harvey probably didn't take his family racing with him, many others did. It was a common site to see family members traveling with race drivers, camping trackside and even working in the pits.

Jim Thornton was one of about twenty-five engineers and drivers with the Ramchargers. They wanted to get Chrysler into drag racing in 1959 and took a scientific approach to it, making many improvements to Chrysler products that resulted in factory support.

Very few Dodge 440 cars were equipped with a 426 Street Hemi and a 4-speed manual transmission. This car is Number 5 of only five produced. Options are scarce on this drag car, which can be driven on the street.

from accidents began to mount. Brushes with law enforcement officials and a negative public image began to threaten drag racers. This led to a movement for a more controlled racing environment and to improve the image of drag racing.

Considerable improvements took place in the early 1950s that would change the future of drag racing. The formation of the NHRA in May 1951 by former dry-lakes racer Wally Parks and fellow racer Ak Miller was a great leap forward. Despite some races moving to abandoned airfields, the NHRA set mandates to control the sport. One of those mandates called for working with law enforcement; another was to organize and control racing events. The effort united various auto racing clubs, and by 1952 the NHRA boasted more than 7,000 members. Rules were established, and classes, together with safety guidelines, established a uniform framework for the sport.

By the 1960s, factory participation was strong in this now-professional sport. Automakers Chrysler, Ford, and GM engaged in strong competition in the Super Stock class, which later became the Stock Eliminator class. The cars ran 400-cid or greater displacement V8 engines. The Dodge or

Ford introduced the 390 V8 into the Mercury Comet in 1966. The twin scoop hood indicates a GT, which could possess up to 335 hp under the hood. The durability run of 100,000 miles in 1963 gave the Comet race credentials.

Plymouth Max Wedge engines dominated the sport in the early 1960s. Engine displacement could range from 413 to 426 cid in the cross-flow "maximum performance" Max Wedge V8s. Dodge Darts and Polaras and Plymouth Furys, Belvederes, and Savoys were some of the cars rivaling Ford and GM. The Chevrolet Impala SS with its 409-cid V8 was another fierce contender, despite being a full-size car. A further GM contender was the rare Pontiac Grand Prix with a 421 Super Duty V8. This was one of the last factory efforts by GM before their 1963 edict to withdraw all factory support from auto racing. The Grand Prix was bested by the fourteen Tempest Super Duty cars built to compete in the 1963 NHRA Experimental class, which was created after lifting the ban on nonstock cars, allowing them to run in their own class.

GM's departure from racing would leave Chrysler and Ford to persevere until the lifting of the ban. Ford had seen poor

Win the running battle for RPM's.

Here a first-generation Camaro launches for the start of a quarter-mile run. The "Christmas Tree" lights have turned green, which means go, go, go! A tree's lights change from top to bottom in a timed sequence before turning green. A good driver will launch the car at the moment the light turns green.

performance from their Galaxy 500 in drag racing events. Armed with a 406-cid V8, these heavy cars were repeatedly bested by Chrysler products with the Max Wedge or lighter Chevrolets and Pontiacs. Ford had decided to develop a real drag car utilizing an existing platform. They used the smaller Fairlane and subjected it to many modifications, resulting in the Thunderbolt. The suspension was heavily reworked to accommodate the large 427-cid V8 into the engine bay. A factory-rated 425 hp was developed by the 427, but was suggested to be as much as 500 hp. Lightweight body panels and a trunk-mounted battery helped to lighten and balance the car. The glass used on these cars was a mixture of safety glass and Plexiglas, which again saved weight and enhanced safety. The Ford Thunderbolts were a success, winning six out of seven divisional titles. In 1964, the T-Bolt set records for elapsed time and top speed at 11.6 seconds and 124 mph.

Muscle cars also exercised their prowess in the National Association for Stock Car Racing. The deep-rooted beginnings of NASCAR are in the Piedmont region of the southeastern United States. This region's population of working-class males would continue to manufacture moonshine well after Prohibition. Even in the 1950s, bootlegging was a profitable but illegal source of income. Men like Robert Glenn Johnson, Jr., or "Junior Johnson" as he is known, worked his father's illegal still in rural North Carolina. He also would become legendary in the delivery of moonshine to customers. Many of these men were drivers and mechanics who modified their own cars for the quick transportation of alcohol while out-running law enforcement or revenue agents. Drivers boasted of their exploits and argued about who was the best driver. This led to many early dirt track races between bootlegging drivers.

Dave Strickler campaigned this 1968 Camaro Z/28 in the NHRA Super Stock Class. He would ultimately win the Super Stock World Championship in 1968 with this car. "Old Reliable" was prepared by Bill "Grumpy" Jenkins and ran times in the 11.70s at 116 mph.

William Henry Getty France, Sr., known as "Big Bill France," cofounded NASCAR in February 1948 and raced against many former bootleggers. Long-standing issues were resolved by adopting uniformed rules and guaranteed purses for drivers and by establishing insurance requirements. Establishing permanent tracks was another priority for NASCAR officials. The first Daytona 500 race held at Daytona International Speedway took place on February 22, 1959. A crowd of 41,000 spectators watched a field of fifty-nine cars and drivers battle for the $67,760 purse. When the race ended, it appeared to be a three-way tie. Ultimately, after watching race footage, Lee Petty was declared the winner by a matter of a few feet. Petty's son Richard later became known as "The King" during the 1949–71 Strictly Stock and Grand National era as well as in the NASCAR Winston Cup Series.

Richard Petty would go on to win seven NASCAR championships as well as many victories to the Chrysler Corporation during the muscle car era. Aerodynamics plays a large role in the high-speed world of NASCAR. Petty really wanted to drive a Dodge Charger Daytona in the 1969 season, but instead drove for Ford. The Daytona was a homologation special; 503 were built to allow its use in racing. The 440-cid V8 was standard, and the 426-cid Hemi was optional. The car was based on the Charger with multiple

The only chance you'll get to pass Richard Petty's Hemi!

Richard Petty's number 43 is known by any NASCAR fan and just about any racing fan. Petty was in the winner's circle at the Daytona 500 in both 1964 and 1966, driving Hemi-powered Plymouth Belvederes.

The Dodge Charger Daytona had great aerodynamic advantages over the competition. The most noticeable addition to the Charger is the large wing. Although they may look the same, the wing on a Superbird has a different height than the one on a Daytona.

DAYTONA "500" Richard Petty pushes his Hemi-powered Plymouth Belvedere to victory at Daytona, Fla., on Feb. 27, 1966.

ROCKINGHAM "500" Paul Goldsmith rocks home to win in his Hemi-powered Belvedere at Rockingham, N.C., on Mar. 13, 1966.

ATLANTA "500" Jim Hurtubise roars into victory lane to take first place with his Plymouth Belvedere at Atlanta, Ga., Mar. 27, 1966.

DARLINGTON "400" Petty again passes the pack to prove Hemi-power in his Plymouth Belvedere at Darlington, S.C., on Apr. 30, 1966.

YANKEE "300" Norm Nelson drives his Plymouth Belvedere across the line to win this USAC classic at Indianapolis, May 1, 1966.

CHARLOTTE "600" In this toughest and longest NASCAR stock car race, Marvin Panch (with relief driver Richard Petty) takes his Belvedere into first place at Charlotte, N.C., May 22, 1966.

Finishing first in nearly every major stock car race this year, Plymouth proves its durability and reliability! On different tracks and with different drivers, Hemi-powered Plymouth Belvederes show they have what it takes to make winners... in races as long as 600 grueling miles.

You couldn't buy one of these cars (specially modified for stock car racing) even if you wanted to. But you can buy a Plymouth designed and built with the engineering excellence that helped make such a record of performance, durability and reliability. Fury, Belvedere, Valiant and Barracuda.

See your Plymouth Dealer today... and take a winner for a test drive!

Ride with the winner... Plymouth

Plymouth

PLYMOUTH DIVISION   CHRYSLER MOTORS CORPORATION

A familiar sight at many NASCAR tracks in the 1960s. Petty's 43 is in the lead, and fans saw his achievements for Plymouth at several high-speed tracks in 1966. "Win on Sunday, sell on Monday" applied moreso then.

modifications. A wedge-shaped nose and tall rear wing were the most obvious features. The nose made the car slip through the air, and the wing provided much-needed down force on the rear tires. This, along with the 426 Hemi, would propel the car to a world closed-course record-setting speed of 199.466 mph in the hands of Charlie Glotzbach at Talledega Superspeedway in Alabama. Daytonas would later break the 200 mph barrier. Seemingly unbeatable, this car was not without at least one design flaw, however. While the wedge nose reduced drag, it caused overheating when driven at slower speeds. This was corrected on the 1970 Plymouth Road Runner Superbird.

The Superbird would help to finally beat Ford's NASCAR supremacy. The Ford Torino Talledega with its Sportsroof or fastback design had dominated the NASCAR circuit in 1968–69. The 429CJ V8 powered the Talledega. Chrysler's Daytona was an effort to stop Ford's domination, but it would take the Plymouth Superbird to renew the battle in 1970. Richard Petty was lured back to Plymouth for the 1970 season to drive these new "aero cars." The adjustable rear spoiler, improved aerodynamics, and torsion suspension assisted Petty in capturing eight of the twenty-one wins for this car. Racing versions had the 426 Hemi, but fewer than 200 street versions were equipped this way. Street versions of the Superbird were hard to sell, with its unconventional looks and large rear wing. Production was just below 2,000 for this single-model-year car. NASCAR rules changed for 1971 against the "aero cars" in an attempt to level the playing field. Only in the fight for a short time, these cars helped to shape racing history.

Historically, muscle cars have been associated with the bad-boy sports of drag racing and NASCAR, but they have a place in a gentlemen's sport as well. The Sports Car Club of America was formed in 1944 as a sanctioning body for road racing and rallying in the United States. Both amateurs and

The famous 1968 Trans-Am winning Z/28 Camaro of Roger Penske was driven by Mark Donohue. It won ten of thirteen races with its Chevy 302 power plant, giving Chevrolet the championship. This car still exists today and is campaigned in historic racing events.

Ford mounted a factory effort in 1969–70 to battle for the Trans-Am championship. The famous Bud Jones led this effort with the talented Parnelli Jones as the driver of this two-car effort. Jones clinched the championship for Ford in 1970 driving his Boss 302 Mustang.

professional racers could take part in these sanctioned events. Their first national sports car championship was created in 1951 based on existing events. In 1966, the Trans-American Sedan Championship was formed at the beginning of the pony car era. This Trans-Am series was designed for

Roger Penske and Mark Donohue both switched over to racing for American Motors in 1971. They were a winning team and won the Trans-Am championship that year in specially prepared Javelin-AMX cars. A special "Trans-Am Winner" decal was available on street versions to celebrate this victory.

THE CLOSEST YOU CAN COME TO OWNING THE TRANS-AM CHAMPION.

commercially produced cars falling into two classes: one for cars under two liters in engine displacement size; the other for those over two liters. The over-two-liter class included many muscle cars: Mustangs, Camaros, Barracudas, Cougars, Javelins, Firebirds, and Challengers would all compete in this class. The less-than-two-liter class consisted of cars from many European makes, such as Alfa Romeo and Porsche.

Several muscle cars were campaigned by factory-backed and independent teams. Roger Penske and Mark Donahue raced Camaros with the unofficial support of Chevrolet in 1968–69. These Camaros in blue and yellow Sunoco livery would win the 1969 Trans-Am championship. Corvette parts bins supplied four-wheel disc brakes with four piston calipers, helping to secure this win. Penske later switched to racing the AMC Javelin and AMX in 1970–71, with several refinements suggested by driver Mark Donahue. The Javelins would win the series in 1971, 1972, and 1976.

A factory effort by Ford created the now-famous Boss 302 Mustang program. The team was managed by Bud Moore, and one of two cars was driven by Parnelli Jones. The Boss was developed specifically to compete in the series. Production cars were known for their reflective decals and the robust 302-cid V8. About 7,000 of these cars were produced for public purchase. The racing version featured a free-flowing Cleveland head; larger brakes and track-prepared suspension enabled this Mustang to lead the pack. The team won the 1970 championship against formidable competition of the Penske AMC Javelins, Pontiac Firebirds, and Plymouth AAR Barracudas.

American racing legend Dan Gurney and his All-American Racers took to the track in prepared Plymouth AAR 'Cudas. These cars were acid dipped to reduce weight and had fiberglass hoods. A destroked 340-cid V8 power plant was not enough to make this car a winner. Budget cuts from Chrysler and a poor fifth-place finish in the championship ended the 1970 season on a last sour note for the AAR 'Cudas. Street production versions were made and could be purchased with a 340 and six-pack induction. A comparable effort was made by Dodge in this series with their R/T Challengers. Dan Gurney's AAR shop prepared these cars for racing as well. One of them ended with a fourth-place 1970 championship finish. The golden age of this series would coincide with the end of the muscle cars in 1972.

Dan Gurney has driven and been successful in several forms of motorsport: Can-Am, Indy Car, NASCAR, Trans-Am, and sports car racing. After his retirement from Formula One in 1970, Gurney was chairman of the All-American Racers until his son assumed the CEO title in early 2011.

"Of all the oils I might have picked—and I've tried a lot of them—," says Gurney, "I settled on the new Castrol XLR racing oil because this multigrade oil is fortified with Liquid Tungsten to give superior performance under the most severe service. I recommend Castrol XLR for any car, racing or not, if the owner really cares about his power plant."

Castrol Oils Incorporated
Newark, N.J., Kansas City, Mo.,
Palo Alto, Calif.

Dan Gurney races with new Castrol XLR Oil the only multigrade high performance racing oil SAE 20 w/50

Castrol is enginuity

A FOXY SOLUTION TO THE GAS PROBLEM.

The Fox by Audi gets about 25 miles to the gallon. Which is about average for an economy car. The thing is, the Fox isn't an economy car. It's a sports sedan. It does 0 to 50 in 8.4 seconds. It has sports car steering and suspension. As well as front-wheel drive. And the fact that you can buy a car that has all this (and more) for only $3,400* provides a Foxy solution to another problem as well.

FOX BY AUDI

*Suggested Retail Price $3399 East Coast P.O.E. (West Coast slightly higher.) Price subject to change without notice. Local taxes and other dealer delivery charges, if any, additional.

THE PARTY'S OVER

JUST AS THE HIGH-PERFORMING muscle cars reached their zenith, several factors combined to bring them to a screeching halt. By 1970, some issues had been building steam against the auto industry for almost a decade. Automakers had been plagued with safety and environmental concerns from lawmakers in Washington, D.C., and consumer advocates (hence the previous bans on corporate-backed racing programs). Insurance lobbyists voiced concerns over the steadily rising auto-related accident and fatality rates in the United States, particularly in relation to younger drivers of high-performance and sporty automobiles. The public's concern and inaction by American automakers to change led to legislation and regulation of the auto industry and America's highways.

In September 1966, President Lyndon Johnson signed the National Traffic and Motor Vehicle Safety Act into law. This would require automakers to provide more safety features in their designs at no extra cost to the consumer. Simple items taken for granted today, such as seat belts for all occupants, energy-absorbing steering wheels, side view mirrors, rupture-resistant fuel tanks, shatter resistant windshields, windshield defrosters, and side marker lights, would be required on all vehicles. This was in direct response to the safety concerns of consumer safety advocates and increasing traffic fatality statistics. Nearly 30,000 people lost their lives in 1965 while driving on American roads. Many of these fatalities included young drivers, and the numbers were anticipated to reach 100,000 annual deaths by the next decade. These were the same drivers to whom the affordable muscle cars most appealed. Automotive industry critics were quick to point out this fact to lawmakers and industry executives.

Consumer advocate Ralph Nader first addressed automotive safety concerns in his 1959 article "The Safe Car You Can't Buy." Nader criticized the lack of safety designs to prevent vehicle crashes and occupant survivability in such a crash. He also pushed the insurance industry to raise their premiums for younger drivers and prevent them from owning performance cars. His 1965 book *Unsafe at Any Speed* focused particularly on the Chevrolet Corvair.

Opposite:
The fuel crisis in the 1970s would drive many buyers away from thirsty V8s and toward more economical imports. The VW Beetle had early successes, which Audi and other imports hoped to build on.

Motorists United was one of many automotive enthusiasts groups that spoke out against government regulation and the Clean Air Act. Many of their concerns about bans on engine modifications and gasoline engines, emissions testing, speed governors, and the auto industry becoming a public utility are still echoed by enthusiasts and the general public in America today.

the DO-GOODERS are killing your car

WITH HYSTERICAL IDEAS & LAWS

FOREIGN CARS VIRTUALLY BANNED IN 1975

AUTO INDUSTRY TO BE PUBLIC UTILITY

BAN CARS UNDER 2,000 POUNDS

ENGINE MODIFICATIONS BANNED

GOVERNMENT TO DESIGN CARS

SPEED GOVERNORS ON CARS

BAN GASOLINE ENGINES

FACTS:
⅔ of smog is not from cars.
1968 and newer cars already emit 70% less fumes.
These controls cost $50 per car, ½ BILLION DOLLARS annually from YOUR pockets. Controls for 1975 standards will cost $200 per car, TWO BILLION DOLLARS annually from YOUR pockets. This money would buy MORE CLEAN AIR by controlling factory emissions.
½ of highway deaths are caused by drunks. Most other accidents are caused by bad driving. Little is being done in emergency driving training, better driver tests, getting drunks off the highway.
Safety gadgets cost $100 per car. Some

of them are not worth the money. Shoulder straps are so inconvenient that only a few per cent of YOU wear them. More convenient shoulder restraints are available.
Better vehicle inspection is needed to reduce smog from older cars, to prevent accidents caused by mechanical defects, and to provide quality checks on automotive service.
Yes, there are problems, but these can be handled with reason, not hysteria.

MOTORISTS UNITED is a new ENTHUSIAST-ORIENTED motoring organization whose purpose is to SPEAK for motorists and influence the government for the

benefit of motorists and the public.
MOTORISTS UNITED are FOR safe, fast, enjoyable transportation, clean air, water and roadsides. Panic programs in Washington, D.C., and Detroit are NOT the answer. They cost YOU BILLIONS OF DOLLARS and cause problems on YOUR cars.

Directors of MOTORISTS UNITED are leaders in engineering, advanced driving, safety, smog control and automotive service; subjects neglected by the other auto clubs. Directors are paid minimum consulting fees. Frequent polls of the membership are taken so YOUR views can be presented.

SEND NO MONEY

Yes, I want to know more about MOTORISTS UNITED.
Fill out, clip and mail to:

MOTORISTS UNITED
Box 384
Washington, D.C. 20044

or: MOTORISTS UNITED
Box 2042
Palos Verdes, Ca. 90274

name

street

city   state   zip

At the time Nader published his book, more than a hundred lawsuits were pending against GM involving the Corvair. Nader pointed out design flaws causing rollovers or spins that easily could have been corrected, but at great expense to GM. Former GM executive John DeLorean later admitted that Nader's criticisms were valid. In 1972, a National Highway Traffic Safety Administration commission report conducted by Texas A&M University concluded that "1960–63 Corvairs possessed no greater potential for loss of control than contemporaries in extreme situations." The report was of little comfort, however, because Nader's book had already made its impact on the auto industry in America.

The year after the National Traffic and Motor Vehicle Safety Act was signed into law, the attention of the public and lawmakers alike turned to the environment. The Air Quality Act of 1967 was the first congressional effort to reduce pollution. However, it set no standards, deadlines, or means of enforcement and was viewed as a failure. This only served to fuel environmental activism. Millions of Americans would participate in the first Earth Day in 1970 and put the environment on the national political agenda.

Due to Nader's criticisms of the Corvair, some owners put his campaign bumper stickers upside down on their cars in protest during his bid for the U.S. presidency.

ECONOMY. PLUS LIBERAL FRINGE BENEFITS.

Good gas mileage is still the thing you want most in a little car, of course. But we know you'd like more.

Like sporty looks and colors and models to choose from.

Bucket seats that fit you comfortably.

Nice soft carpeting.

A floor-mounted shift control and an instrument panel with dials and gauges instead of flashing lights.

Really good handling.

An engine with a little bit of varroom going for it.

A rear seat that folds down and a rear door that opens up, so you can use your little car almost like a station wagon.

The Vega GT.

An economy car-and-a-half.

This year's version of last year's *Motor Trend* Economy Car of the Year. *Car & Driver* Readers' Choice, Best Economy Sedan, '71, '72, '73. *Motor Service & Service Station Management* mechanic survey, Easiest Subcompact to Service, '72. *Motor Trend,* Car of the Year, '71.

VEGA
Chevrolet

CHEVROLET MAKES SENSE FOR AMERICA.

Senator Gaylord Nelson found inspiration from the Vietnam antiwar movement and promoted a national demonstration. The Clean Air Act of 1970 would address some of the activists' concerns.

The addition of safety design features added weight to an automobile, and the Clean Air Act strangled an engine's ability to produce power. This was done by establishing national ambient air quality standards, setting primary and secondary limits of particulate matter, and phasing out leaded fuel. The Environmental Protection Agency identified a number of harmful pollutants to human health: carbon monoxide, nitrogen dioxide, ozone, sulfur dioxide, and lead. Automobiles were required to produce 90 percent fewer hydrocarbons and carbon dioxides by 1975 over the 1970 data. They also were required to produce 90 percent fewer in nitrogen oxides by 1976 over 1971 levels.

The harmful effects of leaded fuel had been discussed for some time. It was first introduced in the 1920s into automotive fuel as tetraethyl lead. Engines produced greater power with the leaded fuel, so there was a reluctance to remove it until required by law. The American auto industry had no recourse but to lower compression ratios to adapt to these new standards while lowering power outputs. Muscle cars had already had their horsepower ratings reduced with the adoption of net versus gross horsepower ratings. Other challenges for the industry included the short time to comply with the standards, the economic impact, and the technological issues to overcome. Many in the auto industry believed the emissions timetables were overly ambitious and unrealistic. Heavy lobbying in Washington, D.C., however, resulted in the extension of some of the deadlines, but an unforeseen conflict

Opposite: The Chevrolet Vega was an effort to capture subcompact sales. It was more of a corporate idea from GM than one that originated within Chevrolet. Early cars suffered several recalls for a variety of problems and hurt GM in the long term.

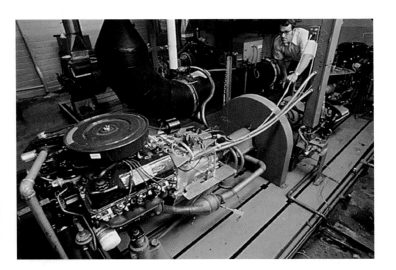

Catalytic converters are commonplace now but were cutting edge in the early 1970s. The U.S. Environmental Protection Agency conducted emissions tests at their national research center to enforce clean air standards. Here they test a Ford Monolith-Honeycombed Catalytic Converter in 1973.

YELLOW FLAG
COMMERCIAL
•TRUCKS BURDEN OF PROOF
•CARS ON CUSTOMER

RED FLAG
CLOSED NO GAS

Left: During the fuel crisis of 1973–74, some states used odd- or even-numbered license plates to determine who could get gas on certain days. Other states, such as Oregon, used colored flags to indicate who could receive gas.

Opposite: Domestic automakers had to fight the growing tide of imports, which were gaining a larger share of the market. Total import auto sales in the United States amounted to 15.9 percent in 1974. Imports provided more fuel-savvy offerings in distinct packages with a growing reputation for reliability.

would force a shift in American automotive focus.

On October 6, 1973, Egypt attacked Israel across the Suez Canal in a surprise offensive. The Egyptians enjoyed some initial success before the Israelis rallied and pushed them back with support from the United States and her western allies. The Arab-Israeli War, or Yom Kippur War, ended when a cease-fire concluded a few weeks later in November. OPEC Arab ministers decided to use oil as a weapon and impose an oil embargo against the United States and allied nations. During this time, 85 percent of Americans were driving to work, and the United States was importing 35 percent of its energy needs. The low fuel mileage figures for most thirsty American V8s and especially muscle cars meant that this embargo was a death sentence. Fuel shortages resulted in some American gas stations running out of gas and prices soaring by 70 percent at the pump. It was not uncommon for cars to run out of gas, abandoned at gas stations in some large cities. Everyone was seeking a more economical and fuel-efficient mode of transportation—not a road-burning, gas-guzzling, high-performance automobile.

All these factors and events led to the demise of the once great and powerful muscle car. Only the Pontiac Trans Am survived, with a 455-cid V8, soldiering on until the bitter end in 1974. It would take almost two decades for the American auto industry to recover and produce fun, high-performance cars again.

New Datsun B-210.
Our economy champion.

Of the 1974 Datsuns, this new B-210 is the most economical. It gets great gas mileage. Upkeep is low. You even save money before you drive it out the door with no-cost extras like rich carpeting, tinted glass, electric rear window defogger, fully reclining bucket seats and power assisted front disc brakes. They're all standard.

Best of all, you get all those saving ways in a really handsome package.

Take your pick of a 2-Door Sedan, 4-Door Sedan or a Hatchback that gives you loads of carrying room in a very sporty body.

Before you pick an economy car, take a test drive in the savingest Datsun of them all. The great new B-210. Drive a Datsun... then decide.

Datsun Saves

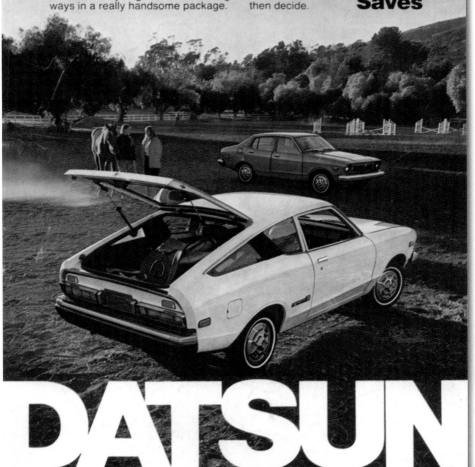

DATSUN

ADDITIONAL RESOURCES

FURTHER READING

Benson, Michael. *Muscle Cars: Thunder and Greased Lightning*. New York: Todtri, 1996.

Campisano, Jim. *American Muscle Cars*. New York: Main Street, 2005.

Gunnell, John. *Standard Guide to American Muscle Car, A Super Car Sourcebook 1960–2000*. Iola: Krause Publications, 2002.

Leffingwell, Randy. *Mustang from Day One*. Osceola, Florida: MBI, 1995.

Mueller, Mike. *Muscle Car Color History: Chevelle 1964–1972*. Osceola, Florida: MBI, 1993.

Statham, Steve. *Pontiac GTO*. Ann Arbor, Michigan: Lowe & B. Hould, 2003.

Witzenburg, Gary. *Camaro: An American Icon*. Lincolnwood, Illinois: Publications International, Ltd., 2009.

Hugger Orange RS/SS Camaros were featured prominently in several advertisements. This convertible is powered by the formidable L78 396 Turbo-Jet developing 375 hp.

PLACES TO VISIT

On any given weekend in the United States, a car show or cruise-in will have its share of great cars from the muscle car era. Many national and international clubs support certain makes or specific models as well. Visit these shows to learn more from owners, or consider visiting their websites and becoming a member. In addition,

This Candyapple Red 1969 Mustang Boss 429 spent several days at Kar Kraft receiving its aggressive NASCAR-influenced conversion. Notice the functional hood scoop and off-center grill badge.

muscle cars can be found in many automotive museums and collections across the United States. Here are a few to consider visiting.

AACA Museum
    161 Museum Drive, Hershey, PA 17033.
    717-566-7100. www.aacamuseum.org
Floyd Garrett's Muscle Car Museum
    320 Winfield Dunn Pkwy, Sevierville, TN 37876-5507.
    www.musclecarmuseum.com
GM Heritage Center
    6400 Center, Sterling Heights, MI 48312.
    586-276-1498. www.gmheritagecenter.com
The Henry Ford
    20900 Oakwood Blvd., Dearborn, MI 48124-5029.
    313-982-6001. www.thehenryford.org
Peterson Automotive Museum
    6060 Wilshire Blvd., Los Angeles, CA 90036.
    323-930-2277. www.peterson.org
Rick Treworgy's Muscle Car City Museum
    3811 Tamiami Trail, Punta Gorda, FL 33950.
    941-575-5959
Volo Auto Museum
    27582 Volo Village Road, Volo, IL 60073.
    815-385-3644. www.volocars.com
Wellborn Muscle Car Museum
    124 Broad Street, Alexander City, AL 35010.
    256-329-8474. www.wellbornmusclecarmuseum.com

INDEX